About *Facing aggression*

Anyone working closely with young people is likely to have to face anger and aggression at some point. Most practitioners will have come across young people who have difficulties managing their behaviour at times of frustration, stress or conflict.

The causes of aggressive behaviour may be deep-rooted and complex, yet front-line staff have to work in the present to deliver services designed for the long-term benefit of those young people.

Facing aggression focuses on strategies designed to enable workers to respond effectively to challenging behaviour—strategies that will enhance their ability to:

- **prevent** incidents of aggression;
- **manage** them effectively when they do arise; and
- **re-engage** with young people, if an incident leads to a break in contact.

Why *Facing aggression*?

Young people, especially those who are seen as disaffected or disengaged, require - indeed, have a right to - sustained and skilled commitment, in order to enable them to change behaviour that may be deep-rooted in their personal histories.

Facing aggression is part of UK Youth's *Working with Angry Young Men* programme. The aim of the programme is to explore how those working with angry or aggressive young men can avoid becoming targets for aggression and maintain their contact with the young person. Whilst we can never fully predict how young people will react, workers can learn techniques and skills that will enable them to achieve this goal.

We see this work as being particularly relevant at this point in time. There is an explosion of practitioners, including learning mentors and Connexions Personal Advisors, whose work is targeted on disaffected young people. Many of them may have little experience of communicating with potentially violent young people.

At the same time, the services many agencies offer have an element of compulsion, which can add to the potential tension in the worker–young person relationship. In these circumstances, agencies must do all they can to build and maintain trusting relationships. It is simply not effective to focus on reasons for *disengaging* from young people and withdrawing services from them.

We must also recognise that some young people have been taught to be suspicious of services and have witnessed those close to them expressing feelings of powerlessness, humiliation or frustration at the services they have received. The result is that they approach our services with deep suspicion. Building trust is not easy. It is, however, the only starting point—and one that needs to be addressed in a purposeful way.

Contents

Facing aggression is in four main sections:

Using *Facing aggression*

Facing aggression is aimed, in particular, at the concerns of **individual practitioners**, especially those whose roles increasingly bring them into contact with 'hard-to-reach' or 'disaffected' young people.

This book will be relevant to youth workers, teachers, youth offending teams, care workers, health workers, foster parents, carers, reception staff, secretarial staff, mentors and volunteers - indeed, anyone who as part of their work has contact with angry young people.

The practical suggestions within *Facing aggression* include tips and techniques to help manage the stress of facing anger and aggression. They are designed to build confidence and prepare workers for some of the challenging situations they may meet.

Facing aggression includes material that can be easily incorporated into **staff development programmes** and training courses. In particular, the *Case studies* section can be used to focus discussion on preventing and managing incidents and re-engaging young people. They can also be used as the basis for role-play for skills practice. The information on *Underpinning theories* provides a starting point for further study and training.

Facing aggression will also be a valuable resource for **agencies** concerned with developing and improving their policies and procedures for minimising and handling incidents of aggressive behaviour—and thus enhancing the personal safety of their staff.

The information included in the *Creating the right environment* section will be relevant for organisations and agencies looking to improve their working environment.

(Case studies in Facing aggression *may be photocopied for training and educational purposes only. All reproductions must include reference to the source.)*

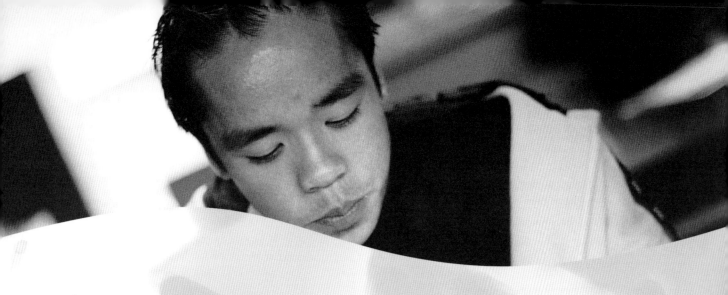

Key principles

The strategies for preventing and responding to aggressive behaviour included in *Facing aggression* are underpinned by a number of key principles for effective work with young people.

The principles summarised here are based on both theoretical concepts and practical experience - they are principles that work in the real world.

Anti-oppressive practice

Aggressive behaviour can often develop from a young person's belief that they are being treated in an oppressive manner. Young people often describe what they consider to be a 'lack of respect' from authority figures. The term 'lack of respect' is usually used to describe perceived discrimination in one form or another.

Where a practitioner does not recognise and address this perceived discrimination, the underlying resentment felt by young person may trigger feelings, which result in withdrawal or serious conflict.

Where practitioners can make issues of oppression explicit, the risk of such situations will be reduced. An example of this would be a practitioner describing to a young person the response of the agency should issues of discrimination arise. This whole aspect of practice requires the practitioner to be open to the views of young people and others on both their own behaviour and on how their agency's way of working can be perceived as oppressive.

Awareness of power relationships

The relationship between the practitioner and the young person is, by its nature, unequal. Being in the more powerful position, the practitioner is obligated to maintain an appropriate relationship. This is essential if we are to help young people acquire the attitudes and skills of a responsible citizen.

We are not suggesting that the feelings and safety of practitioners are less important than the feelings of the young person. What we are suggesting is that, as mature and skilled practitioners, we have more control and greater ability – and, thus, the responsibility – to manage situations of aggressive conflict.

This factor is particularly relevant in the task of re-engaging young people, when relationships are strained. It is often beneficial for the practitioner to take conciliatory action, even when it is the young person's behaviour that has been inappropriate. Embarrassment, fear of humiliation and a lack of social skills make it unrealistic to expect young people to make the first move to rebuild bridges. It becomes therefore, the responsibility of the agency to make contact, where a young person has disengaged from the service.

Promoting informed choice

Young people who feel powerless are more likely to act aggressively.
The more we can work with young people to plan and negotiate mutually convenient agreements - for example the content, timings and frequency of meetings, acceptable behaviour contracts, sanctions for breaking rules etc - the more likely it is that these agreements will be respected and adhered to by young people.

Negotiating with and empowering young people to make informed decisions demonstrate that young people are valued and respected. This is a cornerstone to building supportive and effective relationships. Engaging young people in decision-making minimises the risk of aggression while maximising the possibility of positive outcomes.

Of course there will be certain circumstances within some agencies that are not negotiable - for example court conditions. Non-negotiable ground rules should be clearly communicated to young people when they are inducted into a service, and reinforced as necessary.

Self-control and pro-social modelling

Aggressive situations are usually charged with emotion. Effective practice in situations of aggression requires the ability to think clearly under stress. Practitioners must develop the ability to think through a situation and select the appropriate response, whilst maintaining a view of the longer-term goal.

Through training and experience, an effective practitioner builds a range of skills and techniques, together with the ability to determine which is the most appropriate to use in each situation. The ability to use these skills rests on self-awareness.

By demonstrating self-control the practitioner also has the opportunity to act as a role model for the young person. The term 'pro-social modelling' has been used to describe this approach, which encourages individuals to behave in ways that are pro-social as opposed to anti-social.

Effective communication

We communicate through our behaviour, as well as our spoken words. In usual circumstances, a practitioner has more time to expand and clarify the intended message but, in pressured situations of conflict and aggression, the importance of verbal and non-verbal messages is intensified.

Many incidents of aggression occur due to miscommunication. It is vital that practitioners ensure that verbal messages are clear and understood by the young person. Active listening techniques (see *Underpinning theories* section) are vital tools in reducing the risk of frustration and conflict caused by unclear communication.

As much as 93% of our communication occurs via non-verbal cues - through body language and facial expression. Practitioners need to be aware of the non-verbal messages they may be sending. Verbal and non-verbal messages that are not consistent and appear to conflict with each other can be confusing and frustrating. A good and effective communicator ensures that the spoken word, tone of voice and non-verbal cues work together.

Theoretical understanding

Practitioners require the ability to maintain an objective approach in order to more accurately assess and reflect upon incidents of aggression. Gaining an appreciation of some of the key theoretical frameworks associated with aggressive behaviour is an essential aspect of effective practice.

Placing aggressive behaviour in a theoretical context will minimise the risk of practitioners becoming engaged in personal conflicts. The frameworks can also be shared with young people when attempting re-engagement. This reinforces the idea that the goal is to understand and improve behaviour rather than judge the person.

Some key theories that inform the guidance given in *Facing aggression* are summarised in the *Underpinning theories* section.

Awareness of young people's social development

Young people, by their very nature, are experiencing a process of change and developing social skills. In the successful transition from adolescence to maturity the vast majority of young people discover that the status gained from aggression decreases and the negative longer-term consequences of aggression outweigh any short-term gains.

In this period of transition, many new skills have to be learned and behaviours altered. These include the development of negotiation and assertiveness skills. More significantly, the ability to compromise, deal with embarrassment and accept occasional 'loss of face' are key. Mature adults use techniques of negotiation, assertion and compromise as an alternative to unacceptable aggression.

The process of developing socially acceptable responses to the normal human emotion of anger is complex. It is our role as workers to motivate and equip young people with the skills to consider the consequences of aggressive acts and the long term benefits of substituting non-aggressive alternative behaviours. Young people may then choose to change their behaviour and eliminate aggression.

It is almost inevitable that from time-to-time young people with a substantial history of aggression will relapse and revert to socially unacceptable behaviour. Our role then is to re-motivate, equip and support young people to persevere and maintain changed behaviour to the best of their ability.

Personal safety

For most practitioners, their own safety is not a primary consideration in their day to day work with young people. It is more likely that attention will focus on the many competing demands of working with young people. Often therefore practitioners are under-prepared when aggressive incidents occur.

It is vital that workers and organisations develop habits of personal safety. While this a training issue that cannot be fully addressed in this manual, key issues of personal safety are included in the section *Creating the right environment*, which covers the organisational context of good practice in the face of aggression.

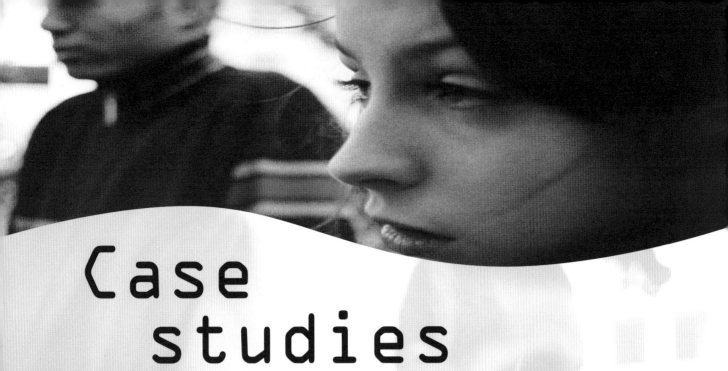

Case studies

This central section of *Facing aggression* uses real-life situations to explore practical responses to aggressive behaviour.

The examples describe situations that lead to aggressive behaviour and, potentially, the withdrawal of a young person from the services of the agency involved. They focus on:
- *In the reception area*: often a focus of conflict;
- *Working one-to-one*: challenging workers' interpersonal skills;
- *Structured group work*: facing aggression in group situations;
- *Referrals and placements*: tensions can arise when a number of agencies are working with the same young person.

Each case study is followed by some suggested strategies designed to enhance the worker's ability to:
- *prevent* the specific incident;
- *manage* it effectively, if it does arise; and
- *re-engage* with young people, if the incident leads to a breakdown in contact.

Notes

While personal skills are essential in managing aggressive behaviour, individual workers require organisational support. The physical and organisational environment required for good practice is covered in *Creating the right environment*.

Case studies are adapted from actual situations. Names have been changed.

In the reception area

An agency's reception area can play a part in provoking young people, who are already distressed or anxious, into becoming angry and aggressive. An inappropriate reception area, or inappropriate behaviour from staff in reception, can cause young people who are initially relaxed and calm to become distressed, anxious and aggresive.

The reception area gives the first impression of your agency. Generally, a reception area that appears friendly, well maintained, colourfully decorated and light will go a long way to promoting the message that service users themselves are valued. A run-down reception area can send the opposite message - a message that can be seen as an invitation to vandalise and disrespect the area.

Waiting times are a major source of irritation. Practitioners and young people alike often feel powerless, particularly when they have no clear idea how long they will be waiting. A young person may well be waiting for a meeting that in itself creates anxiety. A long wait will build tension.

Agencies that take a number of simple steps to improve the reception environment, undertake service risk assessments and train staff working around reception will improve their interaction with young people and reduce the risk of aggression.

As a consequence of the importance of the reception area, the role of the 'gatekeepers' of organisations can be seen as critical. 'Gatekeepers' are a young person's first point of contact; they could be receptionists, but they are also youth club secretaries, coffee bar volunteers, school secretaries, health centre nurses and anyone who answers the phone.

Kept waiting

A worker is late for a meeting

Sam arrives at the Youth Offending Team (YOT) office, and appears to be in a calm frame of mind.

Sam has an appointment to discuss a court appearance and asks the receptionist to see his YOT worker. The receptionist, who knows that the worker is in a meeting and will not be free for some time, asks Sam to take a seat.

Fourteen minutes later, Sam, whose body language is demonstrating that he is getting impatient and agitated, is verbally abusive to the receptionist.

Five minutes later his YOT worker arrives in reception and publicly reprimands Sam. Sam becomes abusive before leaving the building, throwing a chair and kicking the door as he departs.

Sam does not attend court later that week and a warrant for his arrest is issued.

Before - During - After

- What could have been done to **prevent** the situation?

- Once it has arisen, how could it be **managed** effectively?

- How could staff **re-engage** the young person with the service?

■ Before: strategies for prevention

Acknowledgement

A confident or assertive person may have asked the receptionist for clarification of waiting times. Many young people will not have developed these skills. Sam did not feel acknowledged by the service - the receptionist had not informed him of the likely delay. If information had been given to Sam, frustration and aggression would have been less likely to arise.

It may have helped Sam if he had witnessed the call being made to his worker, and then discussed his options with the person on reception. He may have been offered choices, for example, of taking a seat and looking a magazine or going for a walk. It may even have been appropriate to offer to rearrange the meeting. This conversation could have ensured that Sam fully understood that he would need to wait and would have enabled him to say if he had some other pressing issue that would make waiting a problem. This empowerment would have cultivated a positive relationship between the receptionist and Sam, making his abusive response to the receptionist far less likely.

The relationship could have been further strengthened if the receptionist had been empathic, had recognised any concern Sam expressed (verbally or non-verbally) and kept him informed of any progress. If the opportunity had arisen, a deliberately friendly gesture (such as offering Sam a sweet or a drink from the water cooler) would have been more likely to retain a positive engagement during the wait.

Communication systems

Systems that enable the receptionist to advise and update young people about waiting times will assist staff and young people.

Recognition

When the officer eventually does meet Sam, it is vital that the delay is acknowledged. It takes little effort to demonstrate that Sam is valued through apologising for the delay and thanking him for waiting. It is helpful if the worker explains the reason for the delay in a manner that demonstrates that the worker would similarly go out of their way for Sam in a moment of crisis. This builds a solid platform for the session.

■ During: strategies for managing

Reacting to body language cues

Reception staff need to be trained to assess non-verbal cues. If Sam is seen to be getting agitated, there are a number of ways of managing the situation. An acknowledgement that Sam is getting agitated in a manner that is empathic, may nip the agitation in the bud before it escalates. Calling a duty officer may be of assistance; asking the YOT officer to leave the meeting to see Sam may be sensible.

Location and style of intervention

Publicly reprimanding Sam for his behaviour has the effect of increasing Sam's feeling of humiliation and compounding any sense of loss of face. The YOT officer's priority is to assess the risk and, if possible, take Sam away from public gaze and seek to calm him down, using conciliatory words and body language. From here, an assessment can be made about whether to continue with the planned session, to reschedule it, or to arrange a home visit.

■ After: strategies for reintegrating

Follow up is important. This could be through a telephone call or a home visit - usually with a colleague and involving a parent or other significant person as appropriate.

Sam may well have later reflected on and regretted his behaviour, despite any feelings of justification. The agency can take this as an opportunity to apologise to the young person if their expectations have not been met - a gesture that may elicit an acknowledgement and understanding from Sam regarding his own behaviour and the harm that it may have caused. " Further meetings can then be arranged with a greater possibility of Sam committing to a contract of work, enabling a strengthening of the relationship.

Too soon

A young person arrives ahead of time

Freda arrives at the office 90 minutes early for her appointment with her Personal Advisor (PA). It is clear from her demeanour that she is agitated.

Freda has just returned from a planned interview with a prospective work placement but, as the interviewer was away sick, this has been postponed.

Freda's worker is not in the building. Freda continues to demand to see her worker, despite being told that she is out. She then demands her bus fare to return home, stating that this is arranged with her PA.

Freda is told that "no one knows anything about any bus fare arrangement" and that she must come back 90 minutes later.

Freda is verbally abusive to the staff and the service in general, storming out of the building. She does not respond to a letter offering a new appointment for a work placement interview.

Before - During - After

● What could have been done to **prevent** the situation?

● Once it has arisen, how could it be **managed** effectively?

● How could staff **re-engage** the young person with the service?

■ Before: strategies for prevention
Recognise distress and demonstrate empathy

It is important that the receptionist is trained to recognise Freda's agitation and act appropriately. For example, although there are aspects of confidentiality to consider, the receptionist could communicate empathy and concern, perhaps asking open questions or simple inclusive and empowering questions such as: "Are you alright?" This demonstrates friendship and makes it less likely that Freda will be abusive to the receptionist or the service.

If Freda relates her experiences, appropriate empathy can be demonstrated by the receptionist telling Freda that this information will be passed on to her Personal Advisor (PA).

Offer choices

It is appropriate for the reception to call a duty worker to see Freda. Alternatively, many agencies have a buddy system of "back up" workers who share colleagues' caseloads - a familiar face may reduce Freda's distress.

The duty officer, or a trained receptionist can explore options with Freda, given that her PA is not available. Freda can be empowered to decide whether to come back later or rearrange her scheduled appointment. Clearly it should be viewed as understandable, if Freda does not wish to wait or come back to see her PA. If Freda chooses to rearrange her appointment, she should be assured that her PA will make contact at the earliest opportunity.

■ During: strategies for managing
Recognise distress and calm young person down

There is little that the agency can do to reduce Freda's initial agitation - its cause took place elsewhere. However, the agency can seek to defuse her mood. This requires staff training to recognise Freda's non-verbal cues and react swiftly.

A duty officer or paired worker should see Freda. Her argument is not with this agency and this should enable the situation to be resolved without aggression, providing Freda feels heard and has the time and the space she requires to calm down.

Provide practical assistance where possible

Freda is asking for her bus fare home. Although this must be balanced against the perception of rewarding anti-social behaviour, this is a small price to pay for keeping Freda engaged in the service, as opposed to an aggressive incident resulting in the loss of engagement. It demonstrates empathy and is likely to reduce the risk of frustration turning to aggression.

■ After: strategies for reintegrating

The catalyst for reintegration should be Freda's key worker. Freda's key worker was neutral to the incident - she was not there. She should seek to make contact with Freda as soon as possible, for example, by a telephone call or home visit. The visit will be an opportunity to rebuild bridges and re-motivate Freda to seek a placement.

When Freda is calm, the incident can be seen as a learning opportunity - the key worker may employ some self disclosure process such as discussing a time when she felt let down by an interview. Acknowledging the stress of this situation and the normal emotions that these produce can be part of the relationship-building process.

The situation can also be used for 'shuttle mediation' between the receptionist, or staff, who bore the brunt of Freda's aggressive outburst and Freda, making it easier for her to re-engage with the service.

Acting up

Raj's behaviour changes with his mates alongside him

Raj, accompanied by three friends, is waiting to attend his young parents group session at the youth centre. He is usually well behaved in the centre, but on this occasion is loud and challenging. The group remove some leaflets from a display and throw them at each other.

One of Raj's friends start smoking a cigarette. The coffee bar assistant challenges the group. Raj becomes verbally abusive to him.

The senior youth worker is called; she speaks to Raj, telling him that his behaviour can lead to a ban. Raj swears at the youth worker, before he and his friends leave the building, pushing over the leaflet rack on the way.

Before - During - After

- What could have been done to **prevent** the situation?
- Once it has arisen, how could it be **managed** effectively?
- How could staff **re-engage** the young person with the service?

■ Before: strategies for prevention
Provide comprehensive inductions for young people

Raj usually behaves well in the centre. On this occasion he is with three friends, and is behaving inappropriately. Many young people behave differently when with their peers. Embarrassment or the belief that peers expect Raj to be obstructive can promote negative behaviour. There is also the possibility that he is under the influence of intoxicating substances.

The altered dynamics associated with being in a group appears to have acted as a catalyst to the deliberate challenging of authority and the group is unlikely to back down in the face of conflict. A thorough induction, in which the behaviour that is expected of group members is comprehensively explained to Raj, may have reduced the chances of him being accompanied by friends.

Make a friendly concession

A friendly gesture from the coffee bar assistant, such as acknowledging and welcoming Raj on arrival, may reduce the risk of negative behaviour.

A deliberate concession, such as reminding Raj that usually friends are not encouraged and the reasons for this, but that if they behave reasonably an exception could be made on this occasion. This may engender respect and empower Raj to take responsibility for his friends.

■ During: strategies for managing
Adopt face-saving solutions

Raj behaves in an aggressive manner towards the coffee bar assistant and it is important for any staff member in that position to have ready access to assistance. Publicly challenging Raj may not be most effective strategy. If a conflict situation is created, young people are unlikely to accept a public loss of face.

Raj could be individually invited into a separate area, perhaps the meeting room for the young parents group (if this is possible), thus removing the rationale for his friends remaining in the building. If it appeared that his friends are unwilling to leave, Raj could be given some responsibility for resolving the situation, for example, identifying the options available to the agency.

Another approach is to appeal for co-operation and personalise the consequences of the group's behaviour explaining that a particular individual will have to tidy up the reception area after them or that they are 'inadvertently' intimidating others. If the group as a whole are spoken to, it is prudent to be calm, friendly and assertive.

Swiftly see the young person

Engaging with Raj swiftly will reduce the chances of matters getting out of hand. Although it could be viewed as a reward for anti-social behaviour, a pragmatic response may include Raj's involvement in the preparation of the young parents session.

■ After: strategies for reintegrating

An early follow up is needed, if the Raj is to stay involved with the young parents group. The incident has been unpleasant, but Raj is usually well behaved. Should one incident precipitate the end of what had been a positive relationship?

A decision has to be made as to who is best placed to follow up the incident. The follow up should aim to generate a face-to-face meeting. A meeting can be used to condemn the behaviour on the occasion but should not condemn Raj as a person. In fact the usual positive and constructive relationship must be emphasised listening (for more, see *Underpinning theories*).

In the meeting, Raj could be invited to consider who was affected by his behaviour, for example the coffee bar assistant and the other people present. The aim would be to elicit a commitment from Raj to avoid such behaviour in the future. On his return to the sessions, he could be encouraged to make an apology to the coffee bar assistant.

Working one-to-one

Some of the young people with whom we work will become agitated and aggressive in a one-to-one situation. Our experience is that young people with a history of aggression are more likely to view everyday situations as deliberately targeted against them as opposed to 'one of those things that happens in life' and are, therefore, more likely to respond to these situations inappropriately.

Occasionally, young people deliberately use planned aggression (intimidation) where they believe their aggression will gain them an objective - particularly financial reward. Workers who have built positive relationships with young people are much less likely to become targets of this form of aggression.

Aggressive behaviour generated within our agencies is likely to be triggered by situations and behaviours that irritate young people. Examples include:

● being ignored;

● being kept waiting;

● a feeling that the agency has treated them unfairly;

● a belief that the agency has caused them to be deprived of money;

● a perception that the agency has acted in a way to make them 'lose face', such as being placed in a win–lose situation, being humiliated or patronised.

More often, young people will become spontaneously angry, triggered initially by a situation occurring during or shortly before their contact with our agency. Situations that occur before the person arrives at our agency are generally out of our control but, as workers, we need to know how to respond.

Losing out

Gareth doesn't receive the grant he expected

Gareth attends a scheduled meeting with his Personal Advisor (PA).

He is hoping that his PA will secure him a grant to buy the work clothes he feels he needs to start a work placement.

The PA tells Gareth that he has been unsuccessful in his application for funding. On hearing this news, Gareth, who previously had a reasonable relationship with his PA, becomes aggressive and abusive. He makes threats to the service and leaves slamming the interview room door behind him.

He does not return for his next appointment.

Before - During - After

- What could have been done to **prevent** the situation?

- Once it has arisen, how could it be **managed** effectively?

- How could staff **re-engage** the young person with the service?

■ Before: strategies for prevention

Clear communication

Effective communication between Gareth and his PA at their previous meeting could have reduced the risk of aggression. Employing techniques associated with active listening (*for more, see Underpinning theories*) are crucial, for example asking Gareth to paraphrase back the situation relating to the grant. This would ensure that Gareth and the PA had a shared understanding of the process of applying for the grant, likely timescales, chances of getting the grant and what to do if the grant was not obtained.

Deliver bad news sensitively

Bad news can provoke spontaneous aggression. Gareth should initially be invited to sit down (the risk of conflict is reduced if both parties sit at the same height and at an angle to one another).

The PA can lessen the risk of aggression by concentrating on non-verbal body language, such as leaning forward to show concern. This demonstrates that the issue is a shared problem. Care should be taken to avoid coming across as patronising. any use of humour in these circumstances may be viewed as a sign of insincerity.

De-personalise the issue

Gareth may believe that he has been singled out for refusal of a grant. The PA can reduce anger by using language that de-personalises the refusal of the grant to Gareth demonstrating it was an agency decision not a decision about Gareth. Conveying empathy and acknowledging Gareth's frustration is also important.

Consider other solutions

The conversation should centre on exploring other options, even if these are unlikely, demonstrating that the agency remains committed to working with Gareth and providing a face-saving opportunity to close the conversation.

■ During: strategies for managing

Provide space and time

If Gareth becomes aggressive during the interview, we have two choices, either to calm him down or to sort out the problem. Conciliatory and empathic language, body language and an agreement to make further enquiries about alternatives to the grant may provide the breathing space that Gareth needs to calm down.

Take precautions

If we can predict that Gareth may get aggressive, it is imperative that other staff are aware of the situation. This includes taking precautions for our own safety such as inviting a colleague to keep a discreet watch over our interview or, if appropriate, to sit in on the interview. A 'panic button' should only be used if the worker feels they are in physical danger. (More information in *Creating the right environment.*)

If Gareth leaves the building, it is only necessary to take immediate action if he is considered to be a risk to himself or others.

■ After: strategies for reintegrating

Assuming that no physical assault has occurred, it is necessary for the agency to be pro-active and make contact with Gareth. Once Gareth is calm, it will be possible to re-establish a relationship, based on the principle of condemning the behaviour but not the person.

A telephone call, followed by a home or office appointment, usually with a colleague or manager, will help to integrate Gareth back into the service, explore further options and come to an agreement about future behaviour.

Gareth may well reflect on, feel embarrassed about and wish to apologise for his behaviour. Role-modelling by parents, siblings and friends may have taught him that aggression is the only credible behavioural choice when frustrated. Providing an opportunity over time for Gareth to explore alternative behaviours is crucial to his ability to develop the life skills to meet his full potential.

In some circumstances, it may be necessary to change the key worker.

The best laid plans

A worker has the session planned, but...

Richard attends a meeting with his learning mentor. He appears agitated during the meeting.

The learning mentor has planned a detailed programme of work with Richard that day. He does not acknowledge that Richard appears upset, and commences with the work he has planned.

The learning mentor, who has worked hard to prepare the session, becomes upset and frustrated that Richard does not fully engage with the session, challenging Richard with the words to the effect of "I don't know why I bothered preparing this work for you. It's clear you're not listening."

The session finishes shortly afterwards and Richard refuses to attend appointments with a learning mentor again.

Before - During - After

- What could have been done to **prevent** the situation?

- Once it has arisen, how could it be **managed** effectively?

- How could staff **re-engage** the young person with the service?

■ Before: strategies for prevention

Acknowledge non-verbal cues and act appropriately

Richard gave non-verbal cues to the fact that he was upset and agitated. As with many young people, it could be anticipated that Richard did not have the confidence, social skills or depth of relationship with his learning mentor to assertively explain that he was upset and not able to engage in the planned session.

All sessions should start with relationship-building, employing open questions, such as "how have things been since we last met?". Richard may well have responded to sensitive and inclusive questions such as "I can see that something is upsetting you, are you able to tell me about it?".

It is important that the non-verbal language of the learning mentor (tone of voice, posture, seated position) convey empathy and concern. From this, the learning mentor may have been able to assist Richard and come to a shared agreement about whether or when to continue with the planned session.

Offer choices

If Richard is not in the right frame of mind to engage in the session there is no point in continuing no matter how meticulously well planned it is. He can be empowered by the learning mentor to make a decision about the planned session of work. An empowering statement could be "I realise that you have other things on your mind, if at any time you have had enough just say because we can always come back to this." This strategy will allow the relationship to be maintained and ensure that the planned work will get completed at some stage.

■ During: strategies for managing

Provide space to calm down

Provocative language should be avoided at all times. If Richard is agitated, the learning mentor can work to assist Richard in calming down (giving space and time, using open and empathic questions and gestures).

Seek to resolve the problem

If Richard responds to open questions, it may or may not be possible to assist him to deal with the issue that has triggered his agitation. If the matter cannot be resolved, the learning mentor has a responsibility to ensure that Richard does not present an undue risk to himself or others and rearrange the planned session for another date

■ After: strategies for reintegrating

Richard may feel continued anger and resist re-engaging with a service he perceives treated him in a humiliating, unsympathetic or patronising manner.

Although Richard's long-term interests may be best served by continuing to use the service, it would take advanced social skills for him to assert his feelings, and many young people would react by staying away in these circumstances.

It is, therefore, vital for the agency to be proactive in developing a strategy to re-engage Richard. This could include a home visit, possibly involving appropriate third parties for example other workers close to Richard and Richard's family) to resolve a breakdown in the relationship.

If, after mediation, the breakdown of the relationship between Richard and the learning mentor is seen as a blockage to re-engagement this may become a situation necessitating a change of worker.

Too busy

A youth worker is late for an appointment

Davina arrives 10 minutes early for her appointment with her youth worker to discuss her Youth Achievement Award portfolio.

The office administrator on reception notes that she appears relaxed and happy. Her youth worker is 15 minutes late - meaning that Davina has been waiting for 25 minutes.

On arrival, the youth worker makes no acknowledgement of the waiting time. He appears to Davina to be unfocussed and makes no mention of a task that he has asked her to prepare for this meeting.

In addition the youth worker has to leave the meeting on two occasions to take urgent telephone calls.

Davina becomes increasingly sullen during the meeting and, when they are interrupted again, she pushes past the youth worker ignoring his pleas for her to return.

Before - During - After

● What could have been done to **prevent** the situation?

● Once it has arisen, how could it be **managed** effectively?

● How could staff **re-engage** the young person with the service?

■ Before: strategies for prevention

Demonstrate that clients are valued

Where possible front-line workers should demonstrate that service users' are valued by making it a priority to meet them on time.

An acknowledgement and thanks for attending on time is part of a strategy of positive reinforcement, a key factor in building relationships that minimise the risk of aggression. Just as we expect our service users to attend meetings on time, workers should seek to model 'pro-social' behaviour by also being on time and prepared for their meetings.

Acknowledge and communicate when things go wrong

In all likelihood, the youth worker was dealing with an urgent matter. This will happen from time-to-time in our working lives. Davina is likely to respond better to this situation if she is informed in an appropriate manner and in a way that demonstrates that she too is valued.

Even if circumstances are out of their immediate control, an apology by the worker is a powerful tool in defusing aggression. An apology serves to demonstrate respect.

Offer an alternative

Davina can be empowered to make an alternative appointment, possibly offering a home visit or other compensatory measure. This is more likely to retain Davina's engagement in the service.

Organisational systems

As a further alternative, it may have been possible for the youth work team to arrange for a duty officer, paired worker or other colleague to see Davina in *lieu* of her appointment with her youth worker. The duty officer can explain the circumstances to Davina.

■ During: strategies for managing

Time and space

If the planned session with the youth worker or duty worker does go ahead, the first priority must be to enable Davina to calm down. Only when Davina is calm can constructive work take place. Her anger will be exacerbated, if the youth worker unexpectedly has to withdraw, for example to take further telephone calls.

Apology and explanation

An honest appraisal of the situation is necessary and should be discussed with Davina. She is most likely to calm down and resurrect her relationship if the worker acknowledges and apologises for the delay and communicates (within boundaries of confidentiality) the reasons for the delay. Providing the reasons are demonstrated to be an emergency situation (as opposed to undervaluing the service user), most young people will respond well.

Offer alternatives

If circumstances or continued agitation make the planned session difficult, the worker should empower Davina by offering her the opportunity to rearrange the session for an alternative time.

■ After: strategies for reintegrating

It is the responsibility of the agency to be proactive after any meeting, which has not gone to plan. Davina may choose not to re-engage with the service, because she felt devalued and may lack theskills of assertion to make a complaint.

A telephone call, letter or home visit could reinitiate contact. At the next meeting, a further acknowledgement and apology for the agency's role will give Davina a face-saving opportunity to re-engage.

In addition, a deliberately friendly gesture, such as offering to see Davina at home, or go for a coffee may assist to re-establish a relationship and demonstrate that she is valued.

On occasions, relationships between individual service users with individual workers will break down, necessitating a change of key worker.

Structured groupwork

Structured group situations are often difficult to manage and are a common source of aggressive behaviour.

Good groupwork practice requires thorough preparation. An assessment process, which captures relevant information, such as range of literacy skills and levels of motivation, will improve a worker's awareness of the dynamics within the group.

It is essential for group members to have a clear idea of its purpose and what is expected of them. Situations that arise through lack of clarity are difficult to manage, as young people tend to perceive the practitioner as making arbitrary decisions or personalising issues.

It is not uncommon for young people to push boundaries and workers can plan their responses to these incidents. Appropriate staffing ratios create a level of safety for young people and workers.

Workers need to take action, both inside and outside the group, to create conditions that offer equal opportunity and safety within the group. In mixed groups, a balanced group membership (for example at least three Black young men in a group of ten) makes an enormous difference to the potential for developing an anti-oppressive environment. The single member in a group of a particular ethnicity, gender, sexuality etc, is prone to marginalisation and stereotyping.

The materials and the style of delivery will need actively to engage young people. A group that is unfocused is more likely to turn its attention to one another thereby increasing the risk of underlying tensions and aggression.

The stage of a group's development will also affect the likelihood of aggressive incidents. (See *Underpinning theories* for some discussion of this.) Incidents of aggressive behaviour are most likely after the initial forming of the group, at the point that group members are likely to be concerned with status and recognition. The other time when emotions may be heightened is towards the end of the group's life, where some members feel a level of dependency on the group. Other members may then be blamed for the ending of the group.

Confrontation

Two group members confront each other

It is Week Two of a six-week course on interview skills for eight young people.

The group is seated in a circle. The introductory session is successful, although there are one or two moments of tension and the group shows a reluctance to engage in one or two of the exercises. This results in the course running slightly behind schedule.

Tom arrives a little late; the group worker welcomes him and he takes a seat without offering an apology. The worker continues the session but notices that Tom is making gestures towards John, another group member.

The group worker asks Tom to pay attention. He looks suitably attentive, so the worker continues with the session, conscious of time.

Within a few minutes John becomes angry, standing up to swap verbal threats with Tom, who also stands up and begins to leave the room.

Before - During - After

● What could have been done to **prevent** the situation?

● Once it has arisen, how could it be **managed** effectively?

● How could staff **re-engage** the young person with the service?

■ Before: strategies for prevention

Assessment

An assessment process that captures information such as history, levels of motivation and literacy skills improves the worker's awareness of the dynamics of the group.

Aims and ground rules

It is good group work practice to explain the aims of the group and for participants to have agreed ground rules at the beginning of the programme. This allows discussion of behavioural expectations. It also promotes a more certain environment and reduces the risk of aggression.

Explore the issue

The effectiveness of any preventative measures in this case would depend on the reason for the animosity between Tom and John. To prevent the escalation of the incident, after noticing Tom making gestures, the worker could have explored the issue further and reiterated ground rules, which the group had previously agreed.

■ During: strategies for managing

Focus of intervention

As Tom is leaving the scene, an approach to John is more effective at this stage. Tom may well be 'taking time out', allowing himself to calm down. Denying Tom this space may trigger a more serious violent episode.

John is in a position where he could inflame an already tense situation by attempting to follow Tom out of the room. If John is assisted to remain in the room, preferably sitting down, the incident is more likely to be defused.

Style of intervention

It is important that the group facilitator quickly becomes the focus of attention for Tom, John and the rest of the group. This could be achieved by shouting louder than the two protagonists, in the hope that this has a shock effect. There is a risk that shouting will escalate the situation. A more effective method would be to stand close to John, inhibiting the likelihood of further retaliation but not so close as to invade his personal space and compromise personal safety.

The facilitator should ensure that their demeanour and tone of voice do not cause them to become the target for John's aggression. At close quarters it is not necessary to shout, and keeping the voice calm and quiet also assists the facilitator to control their own responses. Only the chosen individual will hear clearly what is said. In addition, being close to an individual allows the facilitator to deflect gestures or words of provocation from others.

The content of what is said can also be important. The facilitator should repeat in their own words the complaints made by John. This is an appropriate and powerful intervention. The complaint will now become a more formal registration of grievance. This technique of paraphrasing allows the release of feelings.

■ After: strategies for reintegrating

It is important to begin the resolution process as soon as possible. In order to reassure and reduce any tension group members may feel following an incident, it is usually helpful to undertake a brief resumé of what happened and take comments before continuing with the session.

Face-to-face contact should be made with Tom as soon as possible after the incident. This contact should initially focus on Tom's motivation for attending the group. Even in groups where attendance is 'compulsory', young people remain in control of attendance. If Tom does not want to attend, his reasons can be explored and further options sought. At this stage, his behaviour in the group can be explored, in the context of it being a barrier to his progress in any setting.

Should Tom wish to rejoin to group, any issues with John should be resolved via a mediation process. At the next session the facilitator should explain to the whole group what has occurred and seek comments from group members before continuing with the work. It is advisable that their relationship be monitored and further discussions should take place if underlying animosity continues to be displayed.

Chain reaction

A worker's response sets off a reaction

It is Week Four of a six-week group for young people in care, coordinated by a health promotion agency.

Lennox joins the group slightly late and, in the process of taking his seat, accidentally knocks over a drink that someone has left on the floor.

The group worker sighs heavily and raises his eyes to the ceiling. Lennox sees this and states that he did not do it on purpose. He becomes increasingly angry and verbally aggressive towards the worker.

Before - During - After

● What could have been done to **prevent** the situation?

● Once it has arisen, how could it be **managed** effectively?

● How could staff **re-engage** the young person with the service?

■ Before: strategies for prevention
Constant awareness

As practitioners working with young people, all behaviour is important, including the non-verbal messages sent. An unintentional non-verbal communication sparked this incident. Such occurrences may be unpredictable and, in this instance, prevention relies on the worker's awareness of all levels of communication.

■ During: strategies for managing
Self-awareness

In the face of verbal aggression, the practitioner is likely to display some of the classic fight or flight responses, increased heart beat, sweating etc. It is therefore helpful for the practitioner to be aware of breathing and attempt to slow their breathing down, in order to remain calm and controlled. In this situation, it is important to be clear that the aggressive behaviour is not seen as an immediate threat to authority.

Verbal and non-verbal communication

Practitioners must recognise that all group members are witnessing their behaviour. This provides an opportunity for pro-social modelling. Urges to move forward and 'face down' young people should be resisted. Taking a step backwards allows greater control of the situation and the worker will be able to see more of what is going on.

Facing down young people is not a technique that can be used with people who are physically much larger than you. It also provides a poor role model for other young people in the group. The stakes will be raised if the worker adds any comments that can be interpreted as win–lose. Defusing the situation and building a constructive group session will not be assisted by inflammatory comments such as "if you hadn't been late in the first place…".

Lennox will be demanding the worker's full attention, so it is essential to demonstrate that they are listening. The folding of arms appears defensive and is usually unhelpful in this situation. To avoid appearing confrontational, the worker should turn their body and head at an angle, slightly away from the conflictual head-to-head position, avoid staring and blink, or intermittently overt their gaze. In this case, the most effective action to defuse the situation would be the offer of an apology and an honest explanation for their actions.

Maintain focus

Making mistakes is a common experience for workers and young people alike. In group situations, less confident young people can easily feel embarrassed and humiliated. In all probability, other young people will attempt to exploit the incident. The role of the worker is to prevent this by stating: "Don't worry about it, we shouldn't have left the drink there - let's continue with the group."

In some circumstances, humour can help to defuse feelings of embarrassment. But, in others, it may prolong a feeling of humiliation, leading to an increased risk of aggression. The group has a purpose, and if minor issues take on unwarranted significance the opportunities for group learning are lost.

■ After: strategies for reintegrating

In our experience, a timely apology for errors and misunderstandings allows potential conflict to be averted. Indeed, this is likely to elicit an apology from the young person too, and rectify a positive relationship. The situation is managed within the group setting and young people remain engaged.

On occasions when the apology is not accepted by the young person it may become apparent that there is a lack of motivation to participate in the group and an incident has been exploited by the young person to create an opportunity to leave. Re-motivating the young person to attend becomes the key task.

Sensitive spot

Anger erupts unexpectedly

A group of young men are undertaking a sport-based groupwork programme.

Having just finished a game of basketball, the group gathers to discuss the benefits of teamwork. They talk about individual scores, as opposed to the team score. As he is not paying attention, Franklin is asked to perform a simple math's sum. He refuses to answer and Ben (another participant) tells him to stop messing about and get on with it.

Franklin becomes instantly aggressive toward Ben, issues threats and leaves the session.

A member of the staff team finds Franklin a few minutes later and it emerges that he cannot perform the task, as he is dyslexic.

Franklin says he is planning to quit the programme.

Before - During - After

● What could have been done to **prevent** the situation?

● Once it has arisen, how could it be **managed** effectively?

● How could staff **re-engage** the young person with the service?

■ Before: strategies for prevention

Assessment

The scope for prevention in this case lies in the pre-programme preparations. An adequate assessment process would have identified Franklin's needs and enabled appropriate considerations to be made.

An effective practitioner should seek to minimise opportunities for participants to experience stigma, as feelings of embarrassment and humiliation are often precursors to aggression and violence.

■ During: strategies for managing

Take the focus

The group leader should respond by becoming the focus for the group thus removing Franklin from the 'spotlight'. Ben too should be kept engaged in constructive group activities.

The group leader could remind others of the established ground rules (for example, respect and confidentiality) explain that there must be a reason for the outburst and that it will be investigated soon. The task of the leader is then to end the session without drawing attention to the subject.

■ After: strategies for reintegrating

In order to re-engage both Franklin and Ben, the group leader (or other worker) should seek to mediate between Ben and Franklin.

There are choices as to the process, for example 'shuttle mediation', culminating in face-to-face mediation listening (for more, see *Underpinning theories*). The matter can be closed as a group issue by taking comments from other group members at the start of the next group, drawing a line under the issue and continuing with the programme.

Referrals and placements

Many agencies assess young people as in need of services or experiences that could best be met by referral elsewhere, for example, through a work placement, support group or specialist drugs or health services.

Young people can develop a comfortable routine using one agency, yet encounter significant difficulties with other services. These difficulties often stem from a natural feeling of anxiety or defensiveness on entering a new environment.

Difficulties can also arise if the referring agency, new service or young person have different understandings of the purpose of the referral, the service that is to be provided and the level of commitment (including behavioural expectations) required by the new service.

New environments can often be a catalyst for aggression or withdrawal. Entering a new setting may cause some young people to feel that they are losing control over something they consider important. The response can be one of anger and frustration. These feelings may be expressed immediately by protest or complaint, often about issues, which appear trivial or unrelated. Alternatively, they can emerge later when a circumstance tests the young person's patience or sense of security. In addition to aggression, some young people respond by withdrawing their participation in services that may be important to them.

Conversely, increased freedom and reduction of external controls can also create tension. For many young people, this can occur when adult supervision is reduced and they feel more vulnerable to intimidation or bullying.

Housing crisis

A homeless young person under pressure
Jaspal is evicted from his hostel for non-payment of rent.

The next day, he attends a city centre youth project and tells a youth worker about his situation. The youth worker speaks to him in her office and arranged for him to attend the local housing department.

On his arrival at the housing department he has to wait for an hour. When a housing advisor eventually meets him, he aggressively demands that his accommodation problem be resolved.

Jaspal is subsequently ejected from the building.

Before - During - After

- What could have been done to **prevent** the situation?
- Once it has arisen, how could it be **managed** effectively?
- How could staff **re-engage** the young person with the service?

■ Before: strategies for prevention
Clarify expectations

It is important to communicate to young people the expectations placed upon them in entering the new environment. Jaspal could have been told about the process that would take place at the housing office, the likelihood of having to wait and the circumstances in which he would have to wait. This can reduce the anger and aggression that stems from frustration or anxiety. It may also be useful to prepare a list, in conjunction with the young person, of what they should say or be expected to know.

Provide information

It is important to provide, with the consent of the young person, information to the external organisation regarding the nature of the young person's needs and any relevant background information. Relevant information should include race, gender and any cultural or literacy needs. Ideally, it is helpful if the young person is accompanied or introduced to a new environment. This allows the young person to observe a model of how to access resources and receive support.

■ During: strategies for managing
Reflect together

Information about the incident should be obtained from the external agency and face-to-face meetings with Jaspal should take place as soon as possible. The aim at this stage is jointly to reflect on the incident, place it in the context of Jaspal's current situation and assess how it has affected his future.

Acknowledge feelings

It is therapeutic for many young people to have their feelings of anger accepted and acknowledged. Resolution of difficulties often results when help is given to describe the source of anger and decide upon the proper course of action. In this case Jaspal would be experiencing a range of emotions that he could be assisted to articulate and place in context. He should then be encouraged to apologise for his behaviour as a starting point for re-engagement with the external agency.

■ After: strategies for reintegrating

The response of some young people to situations where their lives are driven quickly by new events, experience or emotions, is simply to give up. It is, therefore, important to re-motivate and reassure young people who are returning to an external agency.

The external agency may need to be reassured that the risk presented by the young person is acceptable and that additional support will be provided to address any concerns. In an ideal situation, the young person would be accompanied on the next visit to the agency.

Late again

Willis arrives late at his work placement

Willis is in the Fourth Week of a work placement within a painting and decorating company.

His employer is happy with his standard of work, but has spoken to him about his timekeeping, as he has been ten minutes late on two occasions.

That morning Willis is up on time, but his bus is late again and, as a consequence, he is fifteen minutes late. When Willis begins to explain why he is late, his placement supervisor questions his commitment to the placement. Willis becomes angry and verbally abusive to the placement supervisor before storming out.

Shortly after the incident, Willis attends his Personal Advisor's office. After waiting ten minutes to see him, Willis enters the office, sits down and launches into a steam of aggressive and threatening abuse against the placement supervisor.

Willis concludes by demanding to know what the Personal Advisor is going to do about it, stating that he will not cooperate with any further work placements.

Before - During - After

● What could have been done to **prevent** the situation?

● Once it has arisen, how could it be **managed** effectively?

● How could staff **re-engage** the young person with the service?

■ Before: strategies for prevention

Rehearsal

In work placements, it is helpful to rehearse some 'what if' scenarios. The young person could be asked to describe how they would react in particular situations.

Some young people initially feel undervalued and perceive a lack of trust from their supervisor. It may be appropriate to develop some role-plays, for the young person to have an opportunity to practise appropriate social skills and rehearse their responses.

■ During: strategies for managing

Stay in control

Willis is clearly agitated and frustrated. He is seeking a resolution for those feelings. Although the worker was not directly involved in the situation, it is not helpful to react defensively at this point. Empathy is a better response. Even though the worker may feel affronted by Willis's behaviour in their office and wish to respond in an admonishing manner, this is also unhelpful, as it may be perceived by Willis as the e 'final straw'.

Listen

Willis is threatening to disengage from work placements, which may hinder his transition to maturity. At this point, it is a worker's priority to gain an understanding of Willis's perspective. A request that he repeats his concerns slowly will help Willis to calm down. Active listening techniques, such as paraphrasing his responses, will demonstrate that his concerns have been heard.

It is useful to focus on the emotional development of the situation by saying, for example: "It must have been frustrating to sit on a delayed bus when you knew you were going to be late" or "it must have felt unfair to be told off for something that was not your fault." This process will also allow time for Willis to calm down and begin the process of reintegration in a more constructive frame of mind.

■ After: strategies for reintegrating

The starting point for re-engagement is Willis' level of overall satisfaction with the placement. Discussion can focus on the long and short-term consequences of his actions. Willis may feel upset at his treatment, embarrassed or concerned about the loss of face were he to return. This needs to be offset against the positive benefits of completing the work placement.

If after careful reflection Willis is able to identify sufficient positive features for him to wish to continue it is then necessary to identify the barriers that need to be overcome in order to re-start the placement. In addition to an assessment of any risk to, or posed by, Willis at the work placement, contact should be made with the placement supervisor in order to obtain their perspective of the incident and their willingness to restart the placement. If necessary, the personal adviser should advocate on behalf of the young person.

The personal adviser should enable Willis to make the connection between his feelings (frustration at the bus delay, anxiety at the prospect of facing the placement supervisor) and his behaviour (aggression and giving up). It is then possible to arrive at a position where Willis can identify and express a willingness to apologise for inappropriate behaviour towards the placement supervisor.

A review meeting involving the personal adviser, Willis, the placement supervisor and other significant people should be scheduled at the earliest opportunity. This meeting should first seek to mediate between Willis and the placement supervisor. Willis can then be assisted to address any weak points such as timekeeping and enable the supervisor to recognise any particular difficulties that Willis has, for example agreeing a later start time or revised travel arrangements. Crucially, this meeting should also recognise the strengths demonstrated by Willis.

Overload

Workers seem to take over

His key worker at the pupil referral unit takes Curtis to the Drug Advice Centre for an initial assessment on his substance misuse. He is initially reluctant to be referred but, after some persuasion, agrees to an appointment.

Curtis initially becomes irritated when the two key workers spend a long time discussing a recent restructuring of local services. Curtis becomes more agitated during the information gathering part of the assessment, when the drugs worker asks him where he lives. Curtis (who is sensitive about being in care) replies that he lives with his dad. The drugs worker challenges this, saying that he thought that Curtis was on a care order and staying at a children's home.

Curtis becomes aggressive responding with words to the effect of "if you already know everything, why bother asking me these stupid questions". Curtis's pupil referral officer reminds him that he has signed a form agreeing to the disclosure of information when he joined the unit some months ago. Curtis is not satisfied with this and insists on terminating the interview and leaving the building.

It is some months until he agrees to return to the drugs agency to complete the assessment.

Before - During - After

- What could have been done to **prevent** the situation?
- Once it has arisen, how could it be **managed** effectively?
- How could staff **re-engage** the young person with the service?

■ Before: strategies for prevention

Empathy

Curtis was reluctant to attend the Drug Advice Centre. Natural feelings of anxiety will have been heightened in a new environment. Both the drugs worker and the pupil referral officer should have had an understanding that some young people will manage these emotions of anxiety and defensiveness by finding a reason to become aggressive and thus disengage in the process.

Inclusion

The two workers excluded Curtis from the conversation by using the opportunity to 'gossip' about restructuring. Curtis would have felt excluded, undervalued and disrespected. The workers should have concentrated on addressing Curtis's needs and feelings, demonstrating that his attendance is valued and acknowledging that he may feel anxious.

Avoid interrogation

By the time of the assessment, Curtis was in a negative frame of mind. The drugs worker then sought to assess Curtis by asking numerous questions that, in all probability, Curtis will have had to answer frequently, as he is assessed and reassessed by various agencies. Curtis became even more disengaged when he realised that the workers had already discussed the case and knew (or assumed they knew) the answers to many of the questions.

Inter-agency protocol

Other than information directly relating to risk of significant harm, no information should be passed between agencies without informed consent. Curtis will have signed a release of information agreement when he first joined the pupil referral unit. If information is passed *with agreement*, the drugs worker could save time (and Curtis's embarrassment) by explaining the information he has received and asking Curtis to confirm its accuracy. This will allow the relationship to build.

■ During: strategies for managing

Acknowledge feelings

Workers should be able to recognise and acknowledge Curtis's body language. If they have excluded him through their initial discussion they should apologise and acknowledge their mistake.

Facilitate disclosure

If, during a three-way meeting between two practitioners and a young person, one worker is concerned that the young person is not fully answering questions, they could encourage more detailed disclosure by using phrases such as "do you think you are being entirely honest Curtis?" or "do you have anything else to add?" Using an appropriate tone and conciliatory body language avoids the loss of face posed by a 'win–lose' challenge, such as "that's not true", or "you're wrong".

Explain decisions

If information has been exchanged between the workers without prior consultation with Curtis, the worker should find an appropriate opportunity to explain to Curtis why it was felt necessary and helpful to disclose information. The worker should seek to assist Curtis in understanding where this information exchange will assist the agency in best meeting his needs.

■ After: strategies for reintegrating

The issues raised by the meeting should be discussed with Curtis at the earliest opportunity. The worker should acknowledge Curtis's perspective and an apology, where appropriate, would also prove helpful.

Curtis should be informed of and agree to future use and disclosure of sensitive information. A further appointment should then be made to assess him. If he remains anxious about going to the drugs agency, then an appointment at a location where he is comfortable (home, pupil referral unit, youth club) should be made.

Curtis was referred to the drugs agency because the key worker had genuine concerns about his substance misuse. Where a young person perceives a serious breach of trust has occurred, the reallocation of a key worker is worth consideration. Such a course of action would mean time spent building a new relationship. However, this could facilitate re-engagement, as the young person will make a fresh start.

Creating the right environment

If we were to ask young people what they wanted from our services and environment we could expect statements such as:

● welcoming;
● non-oppressive;
● pleasant atmosphere;
● easy to locate and enter;
● short waiting times;
● friendly staff who listen, are easy to talk to and able to help.

If we can provide these, we are taking significant steps in the prevention of aggressive behaviour.

The most important actions that agencies should consider can be divided into the *physical environment* and *agency procedures*.

Physical environment

Reception

A positive, welcoming and high quality environment demonstrates that service users are valued and is most likely to be respected. Generally, a reception area that appears friendly, well maintained, colourfully decorated and light goes a long way to promoting an engaging environment.

Good quality reception areas use appropriate and positive pictures, posters and notices. Signs displaying rules and regulations are important, but should be kept to a minimum. Positive visual and written messages asking service users to refrain from smoking, eating and bringing in friends will be far more appropriate than negative notices, particularly if these ground rules are clearly communicated to young people as part of their induction into the service.

Unfortunately, some young people will interpret a poor environment as an invitation to vandalise and disrespect the area. Vandalism should be repaired immediately. Identified staff should be allocated the task of keeping literature refreshed and inspiring.

Waiting areas should be well ventilated and correctly heated. Reception areas should be arranged so that all clients can be seen by the reception staff. Reception staff should not work alone. Aggression may be inhibited if service users realise that the receptionists are not working in isolation. Reception staff should have an alarm or other systems to summon further assistance if needed.

Some organisations elect to have a glass screen between reception staff and clients. The physical protection of staff must be a high priority of any organisation. There is, however, some evidence that the presence of screens can introduce a 'them and us' perception and make service users more hostile.

Interview rooms

Interview rooms should also be designed to communicate warmth, respect and confidentiality. In addition to communicating the message that the client is valued through the provision of a quality environment, consideration must be given to room layout.

Some organisations choose to bolt furniture down to floors. This, however, can communicate an institutional atmosphere and convey the message that aggression is expected. In providing furniture however, consideration must be given to ensuring that items in an interview room are not likely to become impromptu weapons.

Rooms should employ the minimum furniture necessary to make service users feel comfortable. Many interview rooms are small. A feeling of being crowded can lead to discomfort and anxiety, whereas creating a sense of space can assist young people in remaining calm. Care should be taken with seating arrangements. Service users should always be invited to sit down on an indicated chair.

Evidence suggests that chairs should be at the same level (preventing an image of power differentials). Generally, chairs should be arranged at angles to each other (approximately 45º) and in such a way as the interviewer and service user are not sitting directly opposite each other, which can be perceived as confrontational. Where desks are in the room, chairs at the side of a desk as opposed to across the desk are beneficial.

Seating arrangements should take account of the possible need for escape routes. Generally, when young people become agitated, their instinct is to escape as opposed to attack. Physical violence becomes more likely if young people feel that their personal body space is encroached or that their exit path is blocked.

Ideally, interview rooms should have two outward opening doors, at least one with some form of strengthened glass in it to allow colleagues to keep a check. This enables either party to escape if the situation becomes very difficult. Finally, the provision of a telephone and a (discreet) alarm in easy reach of the interviewer is an important precaution.

Cramped waiting areas and interview rooms increase the risk of aggression. The evidence is that those with aggression problems have a greater personal space comfort zone requirement than average. Invasion of personal body space, which can be exacerbated by seating arranged too close together, can increase feelings of anxiety, which can be a factor making an aggressive outcome more likely.

Sample reception ground rules

Our commitment to you and expectations of you

Waiting times
We aim not to keep you waiting any longer than 10 minutes beyond the time of your appointment, but if it is necessary to wait we will keep you informed about the delay.

If you arrive without an appointment a duty officer will normally be available to see you within 10 minutes. If this is not possible we will inform you.

Code of conduct
Our staff will always treat you with respect. We ask that you treat us with respect. Please make sure that the words you use will not upset anyone.
We ask for your help in keeping the waiting areas pleasant. Please do not eat drink or smoke in the waiting area.

The waiting area is small. You are welcome to bring a parent, carer or one friend with you to your appointment. We do not have the space for your other friends to wait—please arrange to meet elsewhere after your appointment.

Feedback
We are always happy to hear your comments. Comment cards are in the reception area. A duty manager is available if you have a complaint.

Agency proceedures

In addition to a preventative physical environment, it is essential that the agency undertakes a risk assessment covering all aspects of its client contact (reception area, interview rooms, home visits) and draws up procedures for managing risk.

Situations for risk assessment should include responding to individuals or groups who enter the building in a demeanour that indicates that they are already aggressive, clients who become aggressive in the course of their contact with the agency and clients who may provide or become a risk during a home visit.

The protocol needs to establish and ensure that all staff are conversant with risk management procedures (e.g. responding to telephone or alarm calls). As these will be used infrequently and given that many organisations operate with a degree of staff turnover, take students on placements etc, it becomes imperative that procedures are part of staff induction, regularly reviewed and rehearsed.

Where necessary, training may be needed to assist staff from all parts of the agency to assess and identify risky people or situations and respond to them. All incidents that occur must be reviewed by an agency with staff being briefed as to learning points.

Communication systems are key; the recording and sharing of information is important. A service user, who has not previously been problematic in the office or at home, may suddenly become so. At all times it is vital that case records or other recording mechanisms are up to date and available to ensure that no member of staff is exposed to a risk that could be better managed if they have the right information.

Importantly, staff will need to be trained and know what to do if things do go wrong, and have the procedures and confidence to know when to intervene, or summon help.

Policies and procedures can also help to ensure that the agency is consistent. Inconsistencies (e.g. policies on giving money) can cause clients to perceive that they are being treated unfairly and to become upset. Staff training to ensure consistency will assist service users to recognise that the service is fair.

Personal safety

Some examples of personal safety habits include:

- Ensure that colleagues are quickly accessible should an incident occur.

- Having an awareness of the procedures that should be followed should an incident occur.

- Work in areas that permit colleagues to view you if necessary.

- Ensure that there is an unobstructed path for the young person to exit.

- If you feel that your safety is threatened withdraw from the situation and seek support from colleagues.

Underpinning theories

While the contents of this manual are rooted in practical experience, they are also informed by theoretical ideas.

Having an awareness of the underpinning reasons for aggressive behaviour, an understanding of the stages of anger and the types of anger provides the practitioner with a framework for planning and reflection.

Strategies for responding to aggressive behaviour are based upon theories on the nature of communication. Understanding and application of relevant theory will facilitate more effective management and improve personal safety.

This section includes a very brief summary of some of the theories and ideas, which have influenced our approach to facing aggression. It includes pointers towards further reading.

Explaining aggressive behaviour

There are a number of overlapping theories that attempt to explain aggressive behaviour. These theories include: Instinct theory, Motivational/Drive theory, Social Learning theory and Cognitive-behavioural theory. The practice that we have found effective has been based on Social Learning and Cognitive-behavioural theories.

Social learning theorists argue that individuals do not become aggressive because of instinctive urges, motivations or drives but that it is, as the name suggests, learned behaviour.

For a significant number of the young men with whom we have worked aggression has been learned from their parents, siblings, peers and others close to them. For many young people, aggression becomes a defense mechanism to ensure that they are not victimised. For others, influential male role models have actively encouraged aggression as an essential feature of masculinity.

It may well be that, for many young people, aggressive behaviour has proved rewarding. They may have earned what they perceive to be respect and status as well as gaining more tangible rewards. As practitioners who interact with young people we are able to constructively challenge existing beliefs and informally demonstrate alternative responses to feelings of anger and so impact on social learning.

Cognitive-behavioural theory integrates many theoretical concepts to provide the most recent approach to understanding aggression. The cognitive-behavioural model makes links between cognition, beliefs, emotions, behaviour and physiological arousal.

This theory is focused on the dysfunctional beliefs that individuals often hold in relation to aggression. It is concerned with recognising and organising the way individuals think, prior to and during an aggressive situation. It also seeks to identify different methods of coping with stressful situations, linked to the development and enhancement of social skills. Practitioners are in a position to challenge some of the, often negative, perceptions that young people have of themselves and others.

In our practice we have sought also to reflect on aggressive situations with the young people involved with a view to enabling them to understand how the situation developed the implications and consequences of their behaviour and to consider strategies to prevent negative behaviour happening again.

Further reading

Bandura, A. (1973) *Aggression: A Social Learning Analysis*.   Prentice Hall

More, W. (1993) *The ABC of Handling Aggression*. Pepar

Owens, R. (1989) *Violence* Croome Helm

Williams, E. & Barlow, R. (1998) *Anger Control Training*. Winslow Press

Types of aggression

Aggression can be verbal or physical. It is essential to make the distinction between **spontaneous** aggression and **intimidatory** aggression. For the most part, the young people we work with will become spontaneously aggressive after an incident triggers an emotion such as anger. In addition it is important to recognise that some young people, particularly young men, use intimidatory aggression as a means to an end. For example, a young person may intimidate another young person using aggression in order acquire money, goods or improve their own self-esteem. This controlled aggression could become spontaneous aggression should the victim of the intimidation present unexpected resistance.

Further reading

Hopkinson, J. & Rawle, D. (1999) *Understanding Anger - A Groupwork Programme.* UK Youth

Kaplan, R., Konecni, V. & Novaco, R. (1983) *Aggression in Children and Youth.* Kluwer Academic Publishers

Kemshall, H. & Pritchard, J. (1999) *Good Practice in Working with Violence.* Jessica Kingsley

More, W. (1993) *The ABC of Handling Aggression.* Pepar

Owens, R. (1989) *Violence* Croome Helm

Stages of aggression

When recounting an incident of aggression many young people state it 'just happened'. If we work with these young people more closely it will become apparent that there are defined stages that lead to the aggression.

- The initial stage is the **situation**. This is a trigger which can occur in either a private or public situation as in the example below.

- This is followed by an **appraisal**, which is how the person who is likely to demonstrate aggressive behaviour views and interprets the situation.

- The perception of the situation invokes an **emotion**. This could be humiliation, frustration or embarrassment followed by the secondary emotion of anger.

- The next stage is **inhibition**. This relates to how an individual overcomes the internal inhibitors to their behaviour. For example, it is a commonly held notion that men feel a sense of inhibition in relation to physically assaulting women, however, a significant number men also overcome this inhibition.

- The final stage is one of **aggression**, which could range from verbal violence to serious physical assault.

An understanding of this process provides a useful tool when practitioners are reflecting upon incidents of aggression and it can be shared with young people to help them understand their behaviour.

Stages of aggression

Stage	Aggressive Response	Inhibited Response	Agency Prevented
Situation	Tom enters the reception and waits 20 minutes to see his Connexions PA	Tom enters the reception and waits 20 minutes to see his Connexions PA	Tom enters reception and waits 20 minutes to see his Connexions PA The receptionist explains that his PA is dealing with an emergency, sends her apologies and will be with him in 20 minutes.
Appraisal	"It's not fair, I was on time, my PA can't be bothered to see me on time - she's probably sitting around drinking coffee and talking about holidays. My needs are not important to her. I am being made a fool of…"	"It's not fair, I was on time, my PA can't be bothered to see me on time - she's probably sitting around drinking coffee and talking about holidays. My needs are not important to her. I am being made a fool of…"	"It's just one of those things - she would do the same for me if I were in trouble, I'll take the rough with the smooth. I'll go for a walk, or sit here and read these magazines."
Emotion	Likely: feeling of powerlessness, humiliation, tension and stress followed by anger. Emotions reflected by body language and biological changes in body	Likely: feeling of powerlessness, humiliation, tension and stress followed by anger. Emotions reflected by body language and biological changes in body	Unlikely
Inhibition	None: "I don't care."	"I will lose my career prospects, I will look silly, I will regret it later, I might get arrested, my partner will be upset with me."	Not applicable
Aggression	Likely: abuse or assault? Consequence: arrest and exclusion from service?	Less likely: may use passive or assertive behaviour	Not applicable

Further reading

Hopkinson, J. & Rawle, D. (1999) *Understanding Anger – A Groupwork Programme*. UK Youth

More, W. (1993) *The ABC of Handling Aggression*. Pepar

Owens, R. (1989) *Violence* Croome Helm

Williams, E. & Barlow, R. (1998) *Anger Control Training*. Winslow Press

Communication

The importance of effective communication in preventing and responding to aggressive behaviour cannot be overstated. Both verbal and, perhaps more importantly, non-verbal communication can significantly increase or reduce the likelihood of aggressive incidents.

Communication is a process that involves both transference and the understanding of meaning. Communication takes place between a source (the sender) and a receiver. The process is that the sender seeks to encode the message (i.e. convert it into a symbolic form), and pass it via some medium (a channel) to the receiver. The receiver retranslates (decodes) the message, thus transferring the meaning from one person to another.

There are many different channels for communicating a message and many difficulties in both the encoding and decoding stages that can result in the receiver understanding a message at odds with the message that the sender sought to convey.

In order successfully to convey a message face-to-face the sender (encoder) needs appropriate written, verbal and non-verbal skills. In addition the receiver (decoder) needs to have appropriate reading and listening skills.

The Communication Process Model

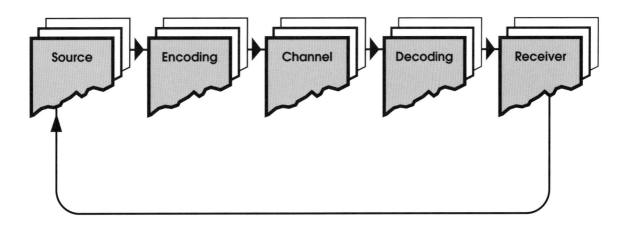

Source: Hamilton, C (1997) *Communicating for Results*, Wadworth

This framework illustrates some key points:

- The practitioner must be clear about the message that is to be sent.

- The recipient of the message will have an impact on the appropriateness of the verbal language used.

- The form of the message must then be decided and in doing this verbal and non-verbal expression must be the same, i.e. hand gestures and eye contact should re-enforce the spoken message.

- It is important that the practitioner gains some acknowledgment that the message is understood. The practitioner summarising the discussion and asking the young person to summarise what they understand can facilitate confirmation of successful communication. (See *Active listening* below.)

There are many opportunities for distortion between the message the sender intended and that understood by the receiver. In particular, issues relating to language, culture, age and gender can cause distortion of the original meaning.

During face-to-face communications, the spoken word can account for just 7% of the received message, with non-verbal communication (tone of voice, eye-contact, facial expression, posture, gestures and so on) accounting for 93% of the received message. Effective communication relies on enabling verbal and non-verbal cues to work together.

Further reading

Argyle, M. (1975) *Bodily Communication.* Methuen

Brody, R. (1998) *Getting Through: Young People and Communication.* Trust for Study of Adolescence

Coleman, J. & Hendry, L. (1999) *The Nature of Adolescence.* Routledge

Hamilton, C. (1997) *Communicating for Results.* Wadworth

Active listening

Active listening techniques are a key method of ensuring that we understand the messages that young people seek to convey to us, and that they understand the messages we seek to convey to them. The techniques are simple, but important to prevent later irritation, anger or aggression, which can be triggered by miscommunication.

Active listening is simply the process of making verbal responses to young people when listening to them (whilst avoiding interrupting, taking over or inappropriately refocusing the conversation). To confirm their understanding of the message, the listener should, from time-to-time, reflect feelings or ideas conveyed, paraphrase the young persons own words or summarise their own understanding of the key points.

In addition to utilising active listening to properly understand and value what young people are saying, practitioners should seek to empower young people to develop active listening skills to ensure they clearly understand the messages we seek to communicate to them.

Further reading

Brody, R. (1998) *Getting Through: Young People and Communication.* Trust for Study of Adolescence

Melia, J. & McGowan, M. (2002) *Working with Young People: Developing Professional Practice in Interpersonal, Communication and Counselling Skills.* Trust for Study of Adolescence

Group development

An understanding of group development theory is important to our understanding of the potential for aggression in structured group situations.

Key to this is the five stage group development framework Forming, Storming, Norming, Performing and Mourning (Tuckman, 1965).

During the **Forming** stage, there may be some aggressive posturing as a defence mechanism but in the main there is little violent or aggressive behaviour between group members as individuals are keen not to upset the *status quo* for fear of being excluded from the group.

During this period, individuals in the group will try to 'sus' each other out and form opinions (some negative) in relation to other group members. Any tensions that occur will generally not surface until the next stage. It is at the forming stage that facilitators can develop the parameters for group behaviour.

It is within the **Storming** phase of the group's life that members begin to confront each other and authority figures as they begin to assert

themselves. This phase of the group's development requires strong leadership, as this will enable the anticipated group conflicts to occur in a controlled manner.

There is an increased potential at this stage for the group members to 'burn their bridges' in order to escape from the pressures created by being a subordinate group member. In order to minimise the tensions and aggression within this phase it is suggested that attention be paid to the make up of the group in relation to race, gender and cognitive ability.

Staffing ratios are also important as this creates a level of safety for young people. During this phase it is also extremely helpful if the available resources and the delivery of such materials actively engage with young people. A group that is unfocused is more likely to turn its attention to one another and thereby increase the risk of underlying tensions becoming aggressive.

While acknowledging that incidents of aggression can occur at any point during the life of the group, the **Mourning** stage can be a very unhappy and distressing time for some group members. Aggression, associated with group closure, may develop as some group members may feel a level of dependency on the group. Potential exists within this stage for members to be blamed for the ending of the group.

Further reading

Doel, M. & Sawdon, C. (1999) *The Essential Groupworker* Jessica Kingsley

Douglas, T. (2000) *Basic Groupwork* Routledge

Hopkinson, J. & Rawle, D. (1999) *Understanding Anger – A Groupwork Programme.* UK Youth

Tuckman, B. (1965) *Developmental Sequence in Small Groups.* Psychological Bulletin, 63, 384-399

Williams, E. & Barlow, R. (1998) *Anger Control Training.* Winslow Press

Wood, M. (2002) *Fundamental – an Introduction to Working with Young Men.* UK Youth

Restorative justice

Restorative justice is associated with repairing the harm caused by behaviour with positive benefits for the victim, perpetrator and society as a whole. Restorative justice can be utilised to resolve a problem, seeking to balance the concerns of the victim and the community with the need to reintegrate the perpetrator back into society.

The focus is on participation and on condemning the behaviour but not the person. Restorative justice can be applied in many ways, for example: restorative conferences, shuttle mediation or face-to-face mediation. The key is for all parties to be given the space to describe their feelings and actions and to fully hear each other's perspectives.

Mediation enables the perpetrator to better understand the harm that their victim has felt and provides an opportunity for a direct apology.

Equally, it enables the victim to hear and reinforce the positive points associated with the perpetrator. Most young people with aggression issues have 'active' learning styles. As mediation demands active participation, this can be a particularly effective vehicle for changing behaviour.

Further reading

Johnstone, G. (2001) *Restorative Justice: Ideas, Values & Debates* Willan

Morris. A. & Maxwell, G. (eds) (2001) *Restorative Justice for Juveniles: Conferencing, Mediation and Circles.* Hart

UK Youth
20-24 Kirby Street
London EC1N 8TS
Tel 0207 2424045
E: info@ukyouth.org.uk
W: www.ukyouth.org.uk

Trust for the Study of Adolescence
23 New Road
Brighton BN1 1WZ.
Tel: 01273 693311
E: info@tsa.uk.com
W: www.tsa.uk.com

Working With Men
320 Commercial Way
London SE15 1QN
Tel 0207 7329409

Young Minds
102-108 Clerkenwell Road
London EC1M 5SA
Tel 02073368445
E: enquiries@youngminds.org.uk
W: www.youngminds.org.uk